Axioms on Leadership

A Companion Guide for Developing Leaders

Michael Ruhl Frank, Ph.D.

Dedication

To my wife Vicky whose support and encouragement have made this work possible.

Table of Contents

Introduction

Teaching someone to lead is like teaching someone to swim – you can show them a movie or give them a book to read, but if you throw them in a pool they drown anyway. You must get in the pool with them, and support them while they flounder, until they finally relax and float.

Why this book?

I was once on a late-night flight from Newport News, Virginia to Washington D.C. during a significant thunderstorm. It was a small twin-engine prop plane with few seats and an open door to the cockpit (it was obviously pre-9/11 days). As I watched the pilot manage the plane through the buffeting storm, I noticed he steadied his hands on his knees and had only the slightest contact with the controls. His calm confidence was at the same time astounding and reassuring. He'd clearly flown through thunderstorms before.

We obviously landed safely, and on landing I asked him how he managed the situation so calmly. He replied that the biggest mistake pilots can make in a situation like that is to overreact to the environment, and that it's important to trust your equipment and crew and to know intuitively how and when to make adjustments. He was also aware of the reaction of passengers to the situation and was intentional in allowing them to see into the cockpit. He understood the situation – not only the system he was responsible for, but also the human factor. His leadership gave us all confidence and reassurance.

Several years ago, with the fall of the Soviet Union, the Army War College developed a concept called VUCA – volatility, uncertainty, complexity, and ambiguity.[1] Basically, the world moved from what was largely a power and threat duopoly to a volatile, uncertain, complex, and ambiguous environment. They needed a framework for how to lead and make decisions in that environment.

Since then, VUCA has become a practical code for awareness, preparedness, and anticipation. In short, VUCA has led to greater focus on situational awareness and decision-making – "management systems" as an essential tool for leaders.

The current environment for business leaders is largely analogous to both flying through thunderstorms and the multilateral VUCA world, and becoming increasingly so with things like the availability of data and information, globalization, and nationalism. Although the advent of "big data" analysis seems to have as its aim the extraction of key information from a complex environment, and I am certainly a supporter of the use of technology and big-data analysis, reliance on it for decision-making may be shortsighted at best and, at worst, may lead to detrimental mistakes.

Data analysis is based on historical evidence.

It's difficult to navigate the path ahead by looking in the rear-view mirror.

My belief is that the development of intuition within leaders is key to both their individual success, and to the success of companies – extraction of intuition gained from experience is as important as extrapolation of data indicators.

How do we prepare future leaders for this environment?

This book is intended to be a companion for people learning to lead. What I hope to do in this book is first, to present clearly and concisely some of the challenges of leadership, and in doing so reassure you that what you may be experiencing has likely been faced before and is not unique to you.

Second, to provide a basic framework and tools for helping to manage those challenges – thereby freeing you to focus on the more important task of leading. This framework is divided into execution and strategy. Here execution is focused on developing a management system, decision-making, and financial acumen. The strategy discussion is focused on taking strategy to action, leading change, and relationship management.

Finally, and most importantly, I provide a section on leading people and introduce the *axioms on leadership* – a set of insights distilled from my experience that will serve as a companion as you develop into a better leader. [2]

There's been plenty of good writing on leadership. However, much of that work requires years of careful introspection and reflection, feedback, and soul searching; or simply emulating the style of a successful leader. Although I'm a big fan of many of those techniques, and have benefitted greatly from them through the years, I've also found through multiple careers that there are, nonetheless, key learnings – axioms – that can be distilled from experience. These axioms are born of successes, but more often failures, and are lessons contained in sayings that I've found myself repeating over and over as I've practiced leadership, and observed and trained others.

I'm not advocating shortcuts – doing the work of introspection and reflection is important. However, one of my goals in the axioms is to hold a mirror in front of you to help make your reflection clearer and thereby accelerate your learning. I believe firmly that *people learn more from discovery than they do from being told.* The axioms are intended to help you discover your leadership ability. You then get to decide if, or how, to apply the axioms to your leadership style.

The approach taken here is intentionally brief and to the point, and my hope is to provide *practical* knowledge. Many of the topics may warrant additional reading. I leave that to the discretion of the reader, and where relevant I've added references to aid in that endeavor. The approach is also intended to serve as a companion – that is, to provide the developing leader somewhere to turn for advice. I've often found value in hearing the experience of someone who's "flown through storms" and understands how to navigate them.

Finally, I would offer a caveat. As you read this book, you should keep in mind that what you're getting is me – my opinions, the axioms according to me, not right or wrong, just opinions. It's up to you to decide if there's value or not, and to develop your own opinions.

The first lesson on leadership is therefore humility, and correspondingly the first axiom is:

Before you can learn you must first admit you don't already know.

And further to recognize that, although you may be the smartest person in the room, you're not smarter than the room as a whole:

None of us is as smart as all of us, and we'll all learn more if we all bring our ideas and opinions to the table, and listen to the views and opinions of others.

Challenges

There go my people – I must find out where they're going so I can lead them.

With that as an introduction, let's begin by discussing some of the challenges of leadership and start with the simple question:

What is leadership?

When I've asked this question of students, I've heard leadership is an attribute like trust or confidence, or leadership is a position – being in front, or the manager of an organization. The conversation I like to have with them begins with; yes, leading is literally being in front with people following you. Leadership, on the other hand, is what you do – your behavior – while you're leading.

Using a boating metaphor, you don't lead by staying in the wake of others, but moving out of the wake means facing the challenges of charting a course through potentially rough or uncertain waters and convincing others to follow you. How you conduct yourself, and how you motivate others, is leadership.

My definition of leadership is therefore:

Leadership is the ability to bring out the best in others (maybe more than they knew they had) to achieve a goal or objective.

What's the difference between leadership and management?

Clearly you need to do both, and in fact without good management skills you are much less likely to become a good leader. There's a very good Harvard Business Review article[3] that basically says that to exert influence you must balance competence and warmth. To understand the point you might imagine the opposites. You might feel compassion for a leader who is warm and incompetent, but you're not likely to follow them. Similarly, you're also not likely to follow someone who is competent but cold or mean spirited. And finally cold and incompetent is simply a non-starter. My intent in this book is to help the reader develop competency in both the technical and emotional aspects of leadership to become a better leader.

I once had an Army officer tell me, "You don't manage soldiers into battle." When you're asking people to give something of themselves – in this case possibly the ultimate sacrifice – it's not simply about achieving metrics. It's about commitment, sacrifice, and trust. You manage things like cost, schedule, risk, scope – you lead people. Leadership is an emotional response – emotional and/or cultural versus mechanical or technical.

A leader without followers is just a person taking a walk.

So how do we learn to lead?

Let's think about the evolution of a leader as chronicled by their changing "mindset" or thought process, and the way they spend their time as the number of people they lead increases.

I once had an organizational leadership consultant[4] tell me that as he listened to individuals or company leaders espouse their values, he would ask to look at their calendars and their checkbooks as a reflection of what they truly valued, or an indication that their values and actions were in misalignment. If you want to know what someone values, look at their checkbook and look at their calendar – it's how they spend their money and their time.

I would contend that in general the way leaders spend their time can be divided into three focus areas: (1) execution; (2) mission, vision, strategy; and (3) people, organization, and culture. As a leader's span of responsibility increases (as measured by the number of people they lead), the time spent on each of these focus areas must also evolve or the effectiveness of the leader will suffer.

Most leaders begin their careers as what I refer to as "individual contributors" – i.e., they have no other people reporting to them and their mindset is, "I am responsible for my own work and performance." The majority of their time is therefore spent on execution, with perhaps some time spent on their own career development and understanding the mission, vision, and strategy of the organization.

Leadership at this level is mostly focused on serving as an example, or being a "thought leader" who influences others through conversation or deeds. It's important to recognize and nurture these individuals for their development and their leverage in guiding an organization.

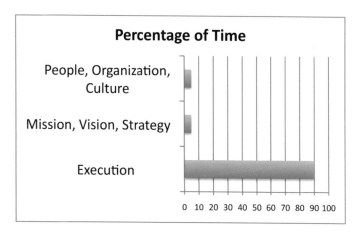

Figure 1: Time management for individual contributor.

The first opportunity that an individual has to lead from the standpoint of responsibility, and the next step in the evolution of a leader, is the first-level manager.

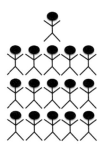

Figure 2: First-level manager.

The mindset of a first-level manager is, "I am responsible for the performance of 15-20 others." This is also the first step away from actually performing work, and the first encounter with what I refer to as the *leadership existential crisis* – i.e., what's my purpose if I don't produce something myself.

I'm reminded of the story of the orchestra conductor[5] who had the epiphany that he was the only member of the orchestra who didn't make a sound – what then was his purpose? After some soul searching, he concluded that his purpose was to bring out the best in others. I would add that there is a system in place – a "management system" – that allows him the freedom to perform that purpose.

Simply put, the management system of the orchestra is the right people are in the right jobs (the tuba player isn't playing violin); every member has role clarity and a clear statement of work that unites the whole (as defined by the sheet music); and the conductor provides the enthusiasm, encouragement, and rhythm for the organization to perform together. This is a useful leadership metaphor, and one on which we'll continue to expound.

The time spent by first-level managers should change correspondingly to focus more attention on people, organization, and culture – and on mission, vision, and strategy to the extent that they need to answer questions from their employees – but they still focus most their time on the execution or performance of work.

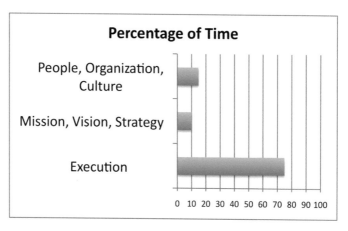

Figure 3: Time management for first-level manager.

One of the key challenges or pitfalls of a first-level manager, which is born out of the *existential crisis* and the pressures of meeting the performance goals of a team, is to become a "super individual contributor" in an effort to carry the team. This becomes a self-fulfilling prophecy by demoralizing the team – "why should we work hard if our boss corrects everything" – leading to more work for the leader, and ultimately causing the leader to spiral to exhaustion.

A properly-constructed management system, as discussed above with the orchestra conductor (right people in the right jobs, role and statement-of-work clarity), will alleviate this challenge and, along with an element of trust and confidence, will free the leader to lead more effectively. It's important to note, particularly for early career leaders, that:

You're only as good as the people who surround you.

You need to surround yourself with people who are as smart or good as you and trust them to do their jobs within their defined boundaries. *Freedom within boundaries* is a theme that we'll continue to revisit as a key to successful leadership.

The next step in the evolution of a leader is what I'll refer to as mid-level management. This is the first opportunity to lead other leaders, and requires again a mindset shift to teaching, guiding, ensuring performance of, and encouraging the organization as opposed to addressing an individual's performance of work.

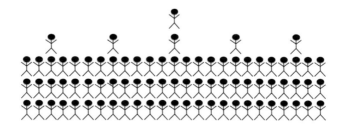

Figure 4: Mid-level manager.

Since the size of the organization is now ~100 people, the granularity of communication changes. And although there is usually no control over the larger strategic direction, there is an expectation for leaders at this level to understand, accept, and communicate the bigger-picture strategy. It is therefore important to develop strong communication skills and financial acumen, and a sense of how to connect bigger-picture strategy to day-to-day activity – the macro-to-micro perspective.

To achieve this, the time investment at this level must also shift to include more focus on organization and strategy. Here again, the leader is moving further away from the actual performance of work, and will continue to face an existential crisis, and will therefore need to balance ensuring work performance with diving too deeply – thereby destroying trust.

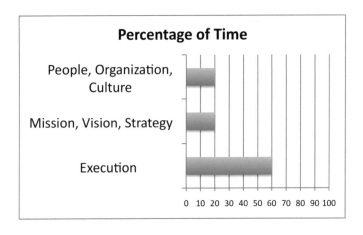

Figure 5: Time management for mid-level manager.

One of the key pitfalls of mid-level managers, and perhaps their biggest frustration, is that although they are frequently responsible for understanding and communicating strategy and ensuring organizational performance, they don't usually have a role in setting the strategy or performance goals. This disconnect can, in some cases, lead to the failure of the individual and their area of responsibility. Again, a carefully constructed management system will help to mitigate this risk.

The next step is the junior executive, and is where leaders by and large have the first real opportunity to set performance goals and measures for their organization in addition to

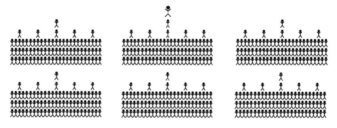

Figure 6: Junior executive.

continuing to communicate strategy and develop people. It's expected at this level that you have developed an understanding of the company's strategy and goals, and you have sufficient financial and strategic acumen to translate that understanding into meaningful goals and measures for your organization. It is a big step from manager to executive, and one that should be preceded by some financial and strategic training.

In my own experience, for example, prior to becoming an executive, I had the opportunity to participate in a two-year program that offered hands-on experience in solving real-world company problems as part of a team. I also attended an executive education course in finance from Wharton titled, "Creating Value Through Financial Management,"[6] and one from the Brookings Institution called, "Inside the European Union."[7] This training was instrumental in helping me become a successful executive leader.

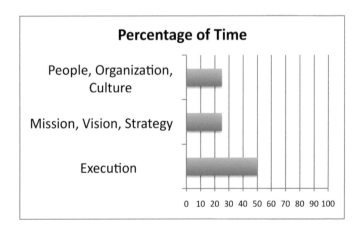

Figure 7: Time management for junior executive.

One of the key pitfalls of the junior executive, which is again a manifestation of the *existential crisis* and the feeling of a loss of control, is the desire to measure too much – overwhelming the organization with metrics. You've probably heard the phrase *what gets measured gets done.* I tend to agree. I would add, however, that *if you measure too much, nothing gets done.*

Metrics should aid decision-making and will drive behavior. It's important to ensure that the behavior that results is the desired behavior and does not have unintended consequences. If the metric does not aid decision-making, then it's a waste of time and a waste of talent within your organization. One likely, and unintended, consequence of over-measurement is the disruption of trust and uncertainty of priorities within the organization.

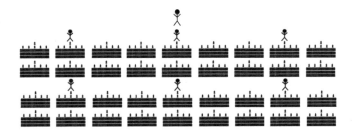

Figure 8: Senior executive.

Finally, we come to the senior executive. From a scope perspective, these roles entail leading a significant portion of a company or business, and potentially thousands of people. All of the previous challenges and pitfalls are likely to manifest themselves here if the corresponding lessons have not been learned.

And as can be seen in the time-management diagram in Figure 9, this is generally the first realization that more time needs to be spent on people, organization, and culture than either strategy or execution.

These leaders are still responsible for setting a vision and strategy, ensuring execution, and, much like the orchestra conductor, putting the right people in the right jobs and providing them with the right structure and resources.

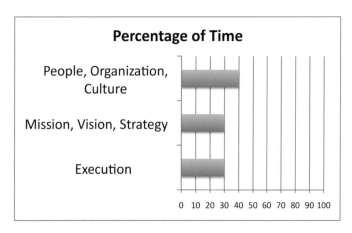

Figure 9: Time management for senior executive.

However, and perhaps most importantly, it is creating the right culture that will lead to high performance and execution. And much like the pilot flying through a storm, carefully measured and applied changes to the controls are essential at this level. Every move has the potential for unintended consequences and a resulting "ripple effect". An organization will react to the actions and temperament of its leader.

One of the key pitfalls at the senior executive level is failing to recognize the importance of culture and communication. The productivity of an organization will suffer if the people are left wondering about things like direction, strategy, priority, or purpose.

Without information people will imagine the worst possible reality.

Execution

Your ability to execute is the price of admission to leadership. However, simply getting the job done is not sufficient – how you do it matters.

Now that we've established some of the challenges or pitfalls of a developing leader, let's assemble some tools to help mitigate those challenges. The structure of what follows is aligned with the time management of the evolving leader starting with execution. The key elements of execution are decision-making, financial acumen, and a management system. We'll discuss each of these in turn starting with decision-making.

Decision Making

The decisions you make, and how you make them, help define who you are as a leader. We must all carry the weight of our decisions.

How do I make decisions?

If you and a group of your friends were contemplating going to dinner, how would you decide where to go? You might discuss type of food, or cost of the meal, or maybe location or quality. These are the criteria for your decision, and they're probably not all equal or equally weighted. Hopefully quality is more important than cost – *I don't care if it makes me sick provided it's cheap!*

In a more formal setting, the decision process entails determining criteria with weight factors for each, and listing the alternatives to be considered. Then by scoring each of the alternatives against the criteria, and applying the weight factors, one arrives at a total score as shown in Figure 10. Generally, this scoring methodology is one part of a *decision brief*.

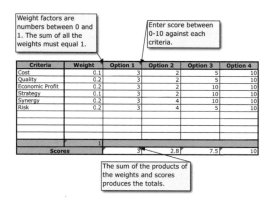

Weight factors are numbers between 0 and 1. The sum of all the weights must equal 1.

Enter score between 0-10 against each criteria.

Criteria	Weight	Option 1	Option 2	Option 3	Option 4
Cost	0.1	3	2	5	10
Quality	0.2	3	2	5	10
Economic Profit	0.2	3	2	10	10
Strategy	0.1	3	2	10	10
Synergy	0.2	3	4	10	10
Risk	0.2	3	4	5	10
	1				
Scores		3	2.8	7.5	10

The sum of the products of the weights and scores produces the totals.

Figure 10: Decision evaluation tool based on criteria and weights.

The purpose of a decision brief is to summarize the thought process behind a recommendation and ultimately a decision. It answers the question of why would you choose one direction over others. The decision brief typically contains the following elements:

- A title page with a brief description of the decision you are seeking.
- A page of background information – situation, relevant context, sense of urgency, why make this decision, what would change, what if no decision were made.
- Alternatives – what alternatives were considered and why.
- The decision model as described above with criteria and weights.
- Risks – this is commonly included in the criteria, but clear understanding of the risks and potential mitigation plans are critical to decision making, as we'll discuss more below.
- Finally, a page of recommendations with reasoning.

I literally mean here that a decision brief is six slides. As someone that has been on both the giving and receiving ends of these briefings, I can tell you that the attention of the decision maker needs to be captured and guided quickly to the most relevant information, while the presenter balances both competence and warmth.

Most of the elements of the decision brief are fairly straightforward. However the treatment of risk deserves a bit more attention.

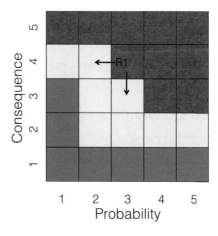

Figure 11: Risk evaluation tool based on probability and consequence. The arrows indicate the results of risk reduction (mitigation) efforts.

A simple risk statement has the following form: *If condition X were to occur, then the consequences would be outcome Y.* The process then is to quantify both the probability of occurrence of the condition X, and the outcome Y. These are typically placed on a risk grid as shown in Figure

25

11. The colors represent the severity of the risk based on probability and consequence. The remaining task is to decide what to do about the risk.

How do risks affect decisions?

The typical actions are to mitigate the risk by somehow reducing the probability or the consequence, accept the risk, or determine the risk to be insurmountable and choose a different alternative in the decision process. The risk assessment and the decision model (criteria and weights) are key elements of the decision process and the decision brief.

Finally, the decision brief serves as a communication device both upward and downward through organizations, and is a historical document for the purpose of tracking decisions.

Financial Acumen

How do my decisions affect financial outcomes?

Financial acumen is a very broad topic, and it is not my intent to cover all aspects here.[8] However, as with our previous topics, there are a few key concepts that I've found particularly valuable in the decision process, and that I believe should be in every leader's tool set. These are the following:

- Cash-Flow Analysis
- Net Present Value (NPV)
- Internal Rate of Return (IRR)
- Weighted Average Cost of Capital (WACC)
- Economic Profit (EP) or Economic Value Added (EVA)
- Return on Net Assets (RONA)
- The Budgeting Process

My treatment of these topics will be to some extent superficial and simplified (the accounting purest may be somewhat dismayed), and I'll focus primarily on why I find them important in decision-making.

Cash-Flow Analysis

In simple terms, cash-flow analysis is examining the cash flowing out of and the cash flowing into a company or organization with some regularity and over some period of time – for example, monthly cash flow for a given year or annual cash flow for a ten-year period. This is particularly important for making investment decisions – obviously companies cannot sustain negative cash flows for an extended period of time without risking financial difficulties.

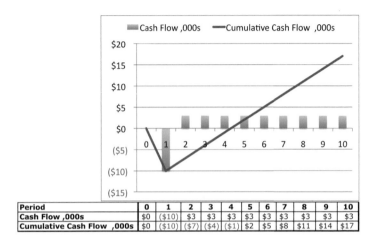

Period	0	1	2	3	4	5	6	7	8	9	10
Cash Flow ,000s	$0	($10)	$3	$3	$3	$3	$3	$3	$3	$3	$3
Cumulative Cash Flow ,000s	$0	($10)	($7)	($4)	($1)	$2	$5	$8	$11	$14	$17

Figure 12: Example of cash flow and cumulative cash flow.

Diagrammatically, cash-flow analysis takes the form of what's commonly referred to as a "hockey-stick" diagram, for obvious reasons, as shown in Figure 12.

Here an initial investment (negative cash flow) has been made with a periodic return (positive cash flow). This type of diagram might reflect, for example, the purchase of equipment that enables a production increase leading ultimately to increased cash flow. It appears, based on the

28

cumulative cash-flow line, that a "break-even" point, or a recovery of the investment, occurs after the fourth period. However, some consideration should be made for the "time value of money", which leads us to the discussion of Net Present Value.

Net Present Value (NPV)

NPV is a mechanism that accounts for the fact that, in general, money received in the future is worth less than money received today. This may be due to inflation or may be the effect of interest if the money was borrowed. We say that the value of money in the future is "discounted" relative to money received today – a dollar in the future is worth less than a dollar today.

To see this, consider the simple one-period example. Let PV be the present value and FV be the future value of an investment with a periodic interest rate R. Then FV and PV are related by the following equation

$$FV = PV(1+R) \qquad (1)$$

If you invested $1000 (PV=$1000) at an interest rate of 10% (R=0.1) then FV is

$$FV = \$1000(1+0.1) = \$1100$$

Similarly, if someone offered to pay you $1000 a year from now, and you generally expect a 10% annual return on your investments, then solving (1) above for PV gives

$$PV = \frac{FV}{(1+R)} = \frac{\$1000}{1+0.1} = \$909.09$$

We see that the present value (PV) has been "discounted" by your expected return (R), which in this case is referred to as the "discount rate".

If we repeat this exercise over several periods, say n times, we arrive at the general equation for NPV:

$$NPV = \sum_{i=1}^{n} \frac{FV_i}{(1+R)^i} \qquad (2)$$

Here FV with the subscript i refers to a value that is i periods in the future and is correspondingly discounted by the denominator (1+R) i times. It's important to note that the future values can be negative or positive corresponding to negative or positive cash flows, and the cash flow is assumed to occur at the end of the period. Fortunately, there is no need to use this formula directly since there are tools like Microsoft Excel that will perform these calculations for us.

In the cash-flow example in Figure 12, with a discount rate R equal to 10%, the NPV would be $6,615.52.

Internal Rate of Return (IRR)

The Internal Rate of Return is simply the particular discount rate (R in equation (2)) that makes the Net Present Value equal to zero. It is, in a sense, the discount rate at which you break even from a NPV perspective. Again, tools like Microsoft Excel will calculate this quantity for you.

The importance of IRR, and it's real utility, is:

If the calculated IRR is greater than your chosen discount rate (your expected return), then the NPV will be positive; i.e., better than the break even point.

In this way, the IRR is telling you how good the investment is, and it is a key discriminator in the decision. In the cash-flow example in Figure 12, the IRR is equal to 26%. If the discount rate is 10%, then we are 16% to the good. For this reason, the discount rate is sometimes referred to as a "hurdle" rate – the rate the IRR must exceed to provide a positive return.

Weighted Average Cost of Capital (WACC)

The Weighted Average Cost of Capital, or WACC, is used to establish the "low watermark" for performance of a company or investments the company makes in its self. It is in this sense the hurdle rate for the company.

WACC is calculated by taking the amount of capital provided by each category (stock, debt, etc.) multiplied by the expected return for each category (a percentage), and finally divided by the total capital provided by all categories. The result is a percent.

Consider the following example: Let's suppose we have $0.6 million in capital from issued stock with an expected return of 10%, and $0.4 million from debt at an expected return (interest rate) of 5%. Then the WACC is given by the following:

$$WACC = \frac{(0.6)(0.1) + (0.4)(0.05)}{1.0} = 8\%$$

Said another way, the cost of capital for each category is the expected return, and the weighting is the amount of capital for each category relative to the total capital. When summed together this gives the WACC, which in our example is 8%.

Economic Profit (EP) or Economic Value Added (EVA)

When businesses provide goods or services they (hopefully!) generate revenue. When we subtract the cost of producing the goods or services we arrive at profit. In simple terms, profit equals revenue minus cost. If we then account for the effect of taxes, we arrive at a quantity called NOPAT – Net Operating Profit After Taxes. If NOPAT is positive, we are led to the conclusion that our business is profitable. However, we're left with the question, "How do our shareholders and creditors feel about our profitability?" They've made an investment in our business and probably have some expected return. After all, they could have made some other investment instead. Maybe they've missed an opportunity.

Does our business create or destroy value?

To answer this we consider the concept of Economic Profit (EP) or Economic Value Added (EVA). EVA measures the profit relative to what might have been the expected return as determined by the WACC. The key point is that our business has invested capital in order to produce goods or services and make a profit.

That capital comes at a cost — WACC — and could've been otherwise invested in something else — like the stock market. So, in terms of a formula, EVA is given by:

$$EVA = NOPAT - WACC(InvestedCapital)$$

or, if we factor out the *Invested Capital,* we obtain

$$EVA = \left(\frac{NOPAT}{InvestedCapital} - WACC \right) InvestedCapital$$

The quantity in the parenthesis is the answer to our question. Our business generated profit (NOPAT) by investing capital. The return we generated, as a percentage, is the ratio of NOPAT to the invested capital. That *return* on our capital must be greater than the *cost* of our capital (WACC) in order to say that we've created value. If it's negative, our investors and creditors might be thinking of making some other investment instead. For this reason, WACC is sometimes referred to as the "opportunity cost".

EVA is a very useful concept for evaluating business decisions and overall business performance. It should be noted, however, that it is *not* the only consideration. In fact, it may be OK for EVA to be negative for some period as part of a larger, longer-term investment strategy. The point is that EVA is a "snapshot in time" – a short-term negative might be offset by longer-term gains.

Return On Net Assets (RONA)

Another financial measure that is frequently used is referred to as RONA – Return On Net Assets. It is generally given by the ratio of the profit generated (NOPAT) divided by the capital used to generate it, and is a measure of how well a business is utilizing its assets. Another way of writing EVA in terms of RONA is given by

$$EVA = (RONA - WACC)InvestedCapital$$

In plain words, in order to say our business has generated value, the return you generate from the capital invested in your business (RONA) must exceed the expected return (WACC).

The Budgeting Process

How do we reinvest in our business?

The process of developing a budget in our personal lives basically entails thinking about our expected income after taxes and our regular, sustaining expenses – like mortgage or rent, utilities, home maintenance, car payment, insurance, and food. And if there's anything left over, we have the discretion to save it or spend it on *discretionary* expenses – like vacations, going out to eat, and home remodeling. If you're like me, there are always more expenses than income, and some method of prioritization and a decision process must be employed. Further, if you fall on unfortunate times, you may need to reduce even sustaining expenses or eliminate assets that generate cost.

Businesses go through a very similar thought process, but significantly more complex – like operating thousands of households each with their own priorities – and it may even require multiple iterations to reach convergence on an executable budget.

In general, each year a business must generate a budget that establishes the required sustaining cost and level of investment that can be made. Unlike our simple household example, the income at our disposal is based on things like forecasted sales and revenue, supplier costs, and desired profit levels. Forecasting sales, revenue, and profit is itself a very tricky task and is beyond the scope of this writing. It depends critically on things like market size, market share, competition, and pricing. One of the seminal texts on this topic is "Competitive Strategy" by Michael Porter.[9]

Our focus here is to help the developing leader understand some of the key considerations and the *thought* process that businesses go through to produce a budget, and how the tools provided in the previous sections are used. We're going to assume that we have a forecasted income that's net of payments to suppliers.

Operationally, developing a budget is straightforward – what income do we have, what expenses do we have, and how do we want to allocate what's left over. We apply the decision methodology and financial analysis of the previous sections and select the best investment options. What's missing from this narrative is the idea that our business must always be evolving – innovating. For example, why should we accept that our expenses are the same or increasing year after year? Our mind set should be to continually question – looking for better, more effective ways of doing business.

The budget process is an opportunity to challenge the status quo.

So how do we do that? The first consideration is to determine whether income is increasing or declining and on what basis is that assumption made – e.g., do we have the necessary capability and capacity to accommodate growth, or do we need to shed capacity with decline. How does our business need to evolve – what elements need to grow (investment cost), what elements are associated with sustainment (sustaining cost), and what elements are candidates for divestiture, sale, or closure.

There are basically two ways to approach this. One approach is based on the belief that our business has been efficient (EVA and RONA are good), and we therefore have a baseline budget to build on from our previous period. In this case we can simply accept the previous period's sustaining cost, account for inflation, and incorporate any discretionary investments that need to be made. This might be an OK approach for a short term during a period of increasing revenue, but in the long term may lull people into inefficiency and missed opportunities.

The second approach, and the one I would advocate, is to start by reconsidering the concept of RONA and the question:

Are we making the most of our asset base or invested capital?

To answer this, I like to think about four elements – capability, capacity, utilization, and condition – and ask the additional questions:

- Do we have the appropriate capability to accommodate the forecasted production?
- Do we have the appropriate capacity to accommodate the forecasted production?
- Are we effectively utilizing the capacity we have?
- Are we adequately maintaining the condition of our assets?

The impact of these questions is easier to understand when we're referring to hard assets like property, plant, and equipment; but I would argue that it applies to labor as well – both "blue-collar" and "white-collar". We can, for example, talk about capability in terms of skills or education, capacity in terms of hours required to perform tasks, utilization in terms of use of overtime, and condition in terms of training or burnout.

It's also important to challenge yourself in answering these questions. Maybe ask yourself and your teams, what would it take to reduce cost by 50%, or what would it take to double our capacity. Sometimes thinking about really hard targets leads to innovation.

Cost-saving innovation frees investment for growth.

The next step is to utilize the tools of the previous sections to organize your ideas into decision briefs. The cash-flow analysis will clearly be a key part of the decision process – what investment (negative cash flow) is required to implement your idea and what return (positive cash flow) will result. It might, for example, be buying a piece of equipment or making a process change. Then by calculating the NPV and IRR, along with consideration of the impact on EVA, a solid financial foundation is generated for inclusion in your decision criteria.

Finally, as you assemble all of the ideas – and the decision criteria – one additional consideration to keep in mind as you decide where to make investments is the core vision, mission, strategy, and values of your business. I mentioned in the introduction that if you want to know what someone values, look at their checkbook and look at their calendar – it's how they spend their money and their time. Your budget is a reflection of what you value.

The decision-making and financial tools of this section are essential to reach an executable business plan. The Management System discussion in the next section is focused on how to make a business plan work.

Management System

Leveraging the power of an aligned organization

A friend of mine who's a retired investment banker once told me, "When you're driving in your car and the road ahead is foggy, you take your foot off the accelerator – and when the road ahead is clear you accelerate." This is human nature. If your employees have a clear understanding of what's important, where you want them to go, and how it ties to a strategy, the productivity will accelerate – visibility accelerates productivity. A good management system creates visibility.

There's a very good Harvard Business Review article titled, "Mastering the Management System,"[10] which advocates that successful strategy execution has two basic rules: Understand the management cycle that links strategy and operations, and know what tools to apply at each stage of the cycle. In that work, the term "management system" is used to refer to the entire closed-loop cycle of strategy development through execution and refinement.

My focus here, and my use of the term "management system," is on the particular task of "operationalizing" a strategy or business plan. What I mean by a management system then is an organizational system of structure, communication, and control that leads to the successful execution of a business plan.

I begin by referring back to the example of the orchestra. The structure of the orchestra provides clear roles and responsibilities – each musician knows where to sit and what music to play and when. The leader (orchestra conductor) then provides the communication and control – unity, rhythm, encouragement, and real-time feedback. The operational part of an orchestra performance becomes automatic, and the leader and the musicians can focus on the higher purpose of leading and performing.

The idea here is to build on this metaphor with the additional element of innovation. Unlike the orchestra, where we're unlikely to change the sheet music of a classical piece in the midst of a performance, we may want to allow some level of innovation within our organization. There may be ideas generated at any level that are worth hearing and pursuing – recall, *none of us is as smart as all of us.*

How do we form an organizational system that provides structure, communication, and control, but allows *freedom within boundaries*?

The first step is to realize that complex organizational structures lead to competing perspectives and/or priorities. The task is to look for places in your organization or business where multiple groups or people are performing the same or similar work. Then, simplify and clarify roles and responsibilities, and align similar functions to the organization structure. This is the thought process in a "matrix" organization. I am a proponent of matrix organizations for the simple reason that it helps focus groups of people on a set of core responsibilities. For example, organizations that are responsible for revenue-producing value streams should not be distracted by administrative tasks – their productivity will suffer, and they're likely to underperform on the administrative tasks.

More specifically, it is frequently the case that individual organizations have people who are responsible for developing financial plans and tracking financial performance. These responsibilities might be better aligned within a single finance "functional" organization to achieve greater efficiency and shared knowledge. In large companies you will likely find organizations like finance, supplier management, and human resources are aligned functionally.

The concept of organizational simplification is particularly important as the organization or company size increases – *complexity doesn't scale well.* There's a very good TED Talk by Geoffrey West titled "The Surprising Math of Cities and Corporations" that further illustrates this point.

The next step is to establish a visibility system or "dashboard" with the following objectives:

- Provide situational awareness
- Connect long-term vision to near-term goals
- Provide a drum-beat rhythm
- Allow visibility of priorities and measures
- Encourage communication and exchange of ideas

The basic concept of a visibility system or dashboard is transparency and alignment. If everyone in the organization has the same information, they're more likely to make good decisions. It's also a very important tool in the shaping of a culture. Allow everyone in the organization to see what the organization is doing and why. As I mentioned in the *Challenges* section: *Without information people will imagine the worst possible reality,* and will waste time worrying.

A simple example of a dashboard is shown in Figure 13. The basic idea is to think about what activities are key to the organization, what results are produced (measures, strategic presentations, etc.), and what information is important to share. These materials should be organized by the frequency they're reviewed. The goal should be focused on decision-making and communication.

	Weekly	Monthly	Bi-Annually
Activity	➢Staff Meeting ➢Employee Roundtable Meeting	➢People Development ➢Metric/Performance Review	➢Strategy Review ➢Business Plan Review
Results	➢Minutes ➢Decision Log	➢People Plan Updates ➢Metrics	➢Strategy ➢Business Plan
Information	➢Employee Sharing ➢Innovation Log	➢Organization Newsletter ➢Company News	➢Celebrate Successes

←――――――― Tactical / Strategic ―――――――→

Figure 13: Example of management system dashboard.

The titles in the dashboard are links to the actual materials. For example, I used a simple Microsoft Power Point slide with links to an underlying file system. That way the individuals responsible for each item on the dashboard deposited their material into the appropriate location in the file system.

I operated my staff meetings directly from the dashboard with the intention that if we needed to see something that wasn't on the dashboard, we'd question its importance and either add it to the dashboard or determine it wasn't important. The dashboard structure made meetings more organized and focused on purpose. Philosophically, I made a habit of asking myself: What information do I truly *need* to see, how often do I *need* to see it, and who else *needs* to see it. Anything beyond that is likely a waste of time for the people producing and reviewing the information.

The value of communication must exceed the disruption it causes.

I once held a meeting early in my career with a significant number of employees. I believed the information that I was sharing was worthy of everyone's time. As I was leaving the meeting, a young engineer was walking out with me and said, "When I leave a meeting, I ask myself if it changed my job or life in some way – and if it didn't, then I shouldn't have been there." I thanked him for his candor, and took his feedback to heart.

Strategy

There are some very good books[11] available on developing a vision, mission, and strategy. What I'm offering here is a simple framework for developing a strategy and seeing it through to action, understanding and addressing the cultural challenges of leading change, and maintaining or managing relationships along the way.

How do we get from vision to implementation?

Strategy to Action

I have a rather simplistic view of strategy. On the other hand, I also believe that strategies are frequently so nebulous that their implementation is nearly impossible.

As illustrated in Figure 14, I believe that once a mission and vision are developed, a strategy is nothing more or less than a roadmap for how to get there. I choose to think that if you can describe your current state objectively and succinctly in terms of a set of attributes, then strategy is how you evolve those attributes over some time frame while leveraging strengths and mitigating weaknesses.

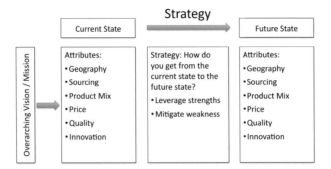

Figure 14: Given an overarching vision / mission, describe the current state in terms of a set of attributes that will evolve to achieve the desired future state.

For companies, the attributes should be closely related to the concept of differentiation – what are the key attributes that you see as differentiators for your company – like product mix, price, quality, innovation. For an individual organization, the attributes should be closely aligned with the company strategy and how your organization fits within the company. Examples might be sourcing, suppliers, geography, and automation.

Converting the strategy into action amounts to:

- Examining the change required in each of the attributes to achieve the desired future state,
- Prioritizing the changes,
- Developing the timeframe (schedule), and

- Invoking a good change management system.

The diagram in Figure 15 illustrates this concept as a "sliding scale."

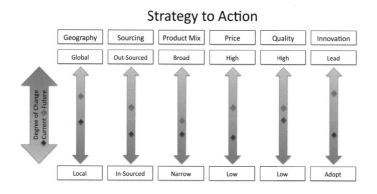

Figure 15: What action will be taken to move the "dot" from the current state to the future state for each of the attributes?

For each of the attributes, think of the extremes or limits, and assess where you would put your business today and where you'd like it to be in the future. In the case of sourcing, for example, it might be that today most of your work is performed "in-house," but in the future you see, as part of your strategy, that more would be "out-sourced." What remains then is to list the specific actions you would take over a specific time frame. These actions can be built into projects and, along with the decision-making tools of the previous section, built into a business plan.

Having said that, I don't mean to underestimate the difficulty of leading change and the challenges of culture. It's been said, for example, "Culture eats strategy for breakfast."[12] These are our next topics.

Leading Change

Leading change is perhaps the most difficult task of leadership. Let's face it; leading the status quo is just not that hard. That's not to say that every assignment is a *change* assignment. The first step in leading change is the discernment of what, if anything, needs to change and why. I've seen too many leaders take a new assignment and immediately start making changes – mostly because they believe it somehow demonstrates their own worth. Change initiatives should be tied to a strategy, and the strategy should live beyond a single leader. The strategy and management system tools of the previous sections can help provide structure and consistency of direction.

I generally divide leading change into two parts – the technical or mechanical aspects, and the cultural or emotional aspects. Both of these aspects have been examined previously,[13] and what I'm offering here are insights that are distilled from studying, experiencing, failing at, and also succeeding at change leadership.

From a technical perspective, leading change has the following key tasks:

- Establish a sense of urgency – why change?
- Develop a vision and strategy – what's changing and how?
- Employ program management best practices[14]
- Create a guiding coalition – *include affected parties*
- Communicate the change vision – enlist thought leaders
- Generate short-term wins
- Ensure rapid-response problem resolution
- Anchor new approaches in the culture

Building these tasks into a management *visibility* system as outlined in the previous sections – whether it's a dashboard or web site, or other visibility application – will help build trust. As previously mentioned, *without information people will imagine the worst possible reality,* and resistance will ensue.

Employ a rigorous management system to instill trust.

The technical aspects of change leadership must be performed rigorously to ensure support, however, the cultural or emotional aspects of change are equally important.

Why is change hard?

Although most people in an organization might agree that *something needs* to change, it's likely that few would volunteer to be the first to *actually* change. This is human nature. The current state – no matter how bad it may be – is known, in some way comfortable, and in it people feel some sense of control. The future state, on the other hand, is unknown, risky, and represents a loss of control. Without addressing this emotional response, change initiatives will be met with resistance. I like to think of leading change in the following context:

Natural selection applies to everything.

What I mean by this is, when a change is introduced into an environment, it is the environment itself that will determine its success.

When something foreign is introduced into our bodies, for example, white blood cells are dispatched to rid us of the invader. Many change initiatives suffer the same fate. The key is to:

Condition the environment to prepare for change.

One way to achieve this is to include representatives of the affected parties – or "thought leaders" – in the planning and decision-making processes.

Create ownership of the future to reduce fear.

Generally speaking, if people can see themselves in the proposed future state, they have an easier time embracing it. I believe this is true even in the case that the future state means a loss of job or responsibility – it's the uncertainty that produces fear, and consequently resistance. The knowledge of what the future entails gives them more of a sense of control and ability to make decisions that affect their own future.

One final note I would offer on leading change is that:

Change is only resisted if it's noticed.

Too often leaders want to make a big splash with a change initiative that may turn out to be barely a ripple. Many change initiatives are more gradual evolution than radical transformation, and the associated communication should be reflective of that. The alternative is an abundance of white blood cells for a surface scratch.

Relationship Management

There are many facets to relationship management, but here we'll focus on three – interpersonal (one-on-one) relationships, network (your relationship with an organization, company, suppliers, etc.), and negotiation (really an activity within the framework of relationship management).

Interpersonal

We'll start with interpersonal relationships. These are generally a question of personality types and how they communicate. There are many personality "evaluation tools" in use – for example Myers-Briggs, Birkman, Herrmann Brain Dominance, and Insights.[15] I have been exposed to each of these – some more than once – and have found that in general they are looking at the degree to which you are introverted versus extroverted, and at the degree to which you rely on logic versus emotion (left or right-brained respectively). I like to characterize these by imagining a coordinate system with axes labeled "Ask-Tell" and "Facts-Feelings" as shown in Figure 16.[16]

The Red, Yellow, Green, and Blue are typical labels for the corresponding quadrants. For example, people who communicate mostly by telling facts (left brain / extrovert) are "Red".

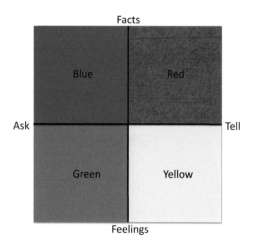

Figure 16: Simple model of personality types.

The general tendencies are the following:

- Red – left-brain / extrovert, tells facts, directive style, decision oriented, decisions based on data, can become impatient when stressed, can appear impersonal, values time.
- Blue – left-brain / introvert, asks facts, generally seeks evidence or data to support decisions, may stress if a decision is required without sufficient data or process, prone to indecision, values data and process.
- Green – right-brain / introvert, asks feelings, generally seeks consensus by asking for and listening to emotional responses of others, may stress if required to be directive or break consensus, values relationships.
- Yellow – right-brain / extrovert, tells feelings, more apt to express pleasure or displeasure with options rather than decide or direct, prone to stress over concise direction or too many details, values loyalty.

These categories are not intended to be good or bad, and every individual is likely to display more than one depending on circumstances. I, for example, am typically Green, but will tend toward Red when stressed. The importance of these characterizations is to understand your own style tendencies, and recognize those of others. This will help you to understand and better navigate conflict. For example, conflicts are most likely to occur with people trying to communicate across a diagonal – asking facts versus telling feelings.

A final point is that with knowledge of your own personality / communication tendencies, as a leader you can develop the ability to move around the coordinate system (adjust your style) to better communicate with your audience. You might, for example, tailor a conversation as, "Here's what I think we should do (Red), I'm excited about it (Yellow), how do you feel (Green), and what do you need from me to get it done (Blue)." You have effectively moved through all four quadrants.

Networks

It's often said that to be a successful leader you must have a strong network. But seldom do you hear someone describe how to develop or use a network – what it is, how it is structured.

Why have a network?

From a career perspective, without a network it's frequently difficult to be noticed regardless of the quality of your work or expertise – particularly in a large company. I always told people whom I mentored that moving up in a large company requires first, that you're really good at your current job. Think about the mistake of the football receiver who starts to run before catching the pass – focusing on the next task before completing the one you're on is a mistake. And second, become visible – if you're not visible, your hard work won't be noticed. That's where networks can help.

More generally, in business, a network provides an alternative or lever to pull, for example, in the event of process failures or unforeseen problems. The ability to make a phone call to individuals in your network can quickly resolve a problem before it becomes a crisis. In logistics, for example, contacting suppliers, shipping companies, and production leaders to reprioritize supplier deliveries, shipping methods, and production assembly might mitigate a part shortage.

It would be a mistake, however, to rely solely on a network of relationships to run a business. The business would be prone to failure at the loss of key people, or disconnects in relationships.

In a business, you can embed knowledge in people or in processes – the former creates risk.

If you see your business depending on networks as a norm, you may want to pursue a more process-balanced approach.

My take on a network is simple:

A network is a structure of relationships you turn to when appropriate to seek feedback and influence outcomes.

The key words here are *appropriate, feedback, and influence.* Appropriate use of a network is a matter of ethics and sincerity – use your network for the right reasons and at the right frequency. Overuse or ethics violations are career "derailers." Seeking feedback sincerely from multiple people and levels provides valuable awareness. Finally, and quite honestly, the primary purpose of a network is influence, and is a concept that offers guidance for how we can structure it.

Begin by considering areas that are influenced – like your career, your organization, the company more broadly, suppliers, or customers. Next think about key people – *influencers* – in each category and begin constructing a network diagram.

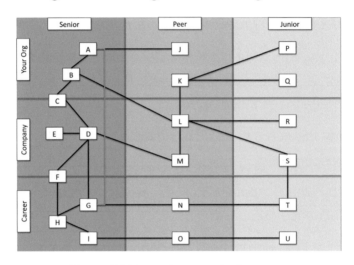

Figure 17: Example network diagram.

The diagram in Figure 17 is a simple example (you may think of other ways to visualize your network). The rows and columns in the diagram represent the areas that are influenced and the levels of individuals in those areas relative to your position. The alphabetically labeled boxes represent the names of individuals you'd like to have in your network. The lines represent relationships each of them has within your network – recognizing that people within your network likely talk with each other too. The number of lines attached to a given box is an indication of how "well connected" an individual might be.

The action then is to select a few of the key connection points and reach out to these people at times when there is no problem – develop an on-going relationship. The initial purpose might be informal conversation about your area of responsibility in the context of the company and how it relates to their area of responsibility. Or in the case of your career, the purpose is mentoring and/or feedback.

The key is to make these conversations informal, but be prepared to bring something of value to the table – something that you can do above-and-beyond to help their organization or their job. It's a two-way street – your influence might help them as well.

It's also important to remember influencers within your organization. These are people who report to you – *thought leaders* – whom others look to for their opinions. Keeping them in your network and maintaining an open, candid communication channel is essential to understanding the underlying tone and culture of your organization – particularly in the case of larger organizations.

Negotiations

Negotiations occur frequently in business and in life – both formally and informally. One of the more common mistakes is to think of a negotiation as a one-time event rather than part of an on-going relationship – a series of negotiations taking place over multiple years or contracts. Preservation of a relationship may, in fact, be as important as achieving a particular goal. We always need to keep in mind what the measures of success are, and how our success today might affect the next negotiation.

What's the ultimate goal?

In any case, unless you are certain the negotiation is a "once-and-done," it is best to look for a "win-win" solution; i.e., one in which both sides feel they have achieved some level of success, and to think of a negotiation as one event in a series and part of an on-going relationship.

To that end, I like to think of negotiations as having four aspects – long-term goals, desired outcomes, required outcomes, and leverage. And it's important to understand these aspects for both sides of the negotiation. A sliding scale diagram, as was used in our Strategy to Action discussion, can once again be used to capture this thought process as shown in Figure 18.

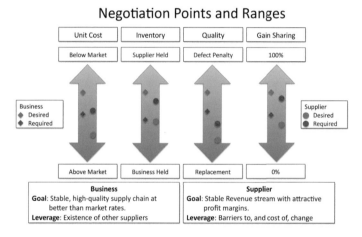

Figure 18: Where are the gaps and overlaps in the key negotiation points?

The scenario in the Figure 18 considers a relationship between a business and a supplier (let's say the supplier provides a physical part of some kind). The key negotiation points in this example are unit cost, inventory, quality, and gain sharing. The position of the business (in this case you) and the anticipated position of the supplier are represented by the diamonds and circles respectively. The long-term goal and leverage are also listed for each. The utility of the diagram is that it helps frame the relative positions and basis for negotiation in a simple representation.

For example: It appears that there is very little negotiation room on unit price, but there is some overlap. On the other hand, there is significant overlap on how inventory is held (supplier-held inventory might help reduce your cost) and the concept of gain sharing (e.g., when the supplier implements good ideas that lower their cost, your business gets a share – you may even contribute ideas or help them with implementation). These might be easy wins for both sides, and might be used as leverage to help with more difficult areas.

Finally, in the area of quality, it appears that there is likely no appetite by the supplier to pay a penalty for quality defects. This may be one of those areas where you consider your long-term goal and leverage, and the value of the relationship in gauging how hard to push this point.

The key point in this discussion is to have a clear idea of your position (long-term goals, desired outcomes, required outcomes, and leverage) and that of your counterpart prior to entering into a negotiation. The tool offered here is one way of framing those positions to facilitate your understanding of how to proceed in the negotiation.

Leading People

The sections on Execution and Strategy were intended to help the developing leader increase competency in *managing* an organization. Achieving a level of mastery in those concepts gives a leader the freedom to focus on the more-important task of *leading* people. As shown in the time management diagrams in the Challenges section, people-leadership skills become more and more important as the level of leadership responsibility increases.

Throughout the previous sections, I've left "bread crumbs" that guide us to this section. Our focus here is on the rather *subjective* topic of leading people. I can't simply *tell* you how to lead. The approach taken is to present you with statements that, hopefully, provoke thought, introspection, and discovery – *people learn more from discovery than they do from being told.*

We begin by recalling our working definition of leadership:

Leadership is the ability to bring out the best in others (maybe more than they knew they had) to achieve a goal or objective.

In order to achieve this, people must *believe* in you – *trust* in both your ability and in your caring for them. Good leaders have the ability to draw on, or leverage, an emotional response. My belief is, further, that the best leaders are those who know themselves and have an understanding of, and compassion for, human nature.

Axioms on Leadership

In simple terms, an *axiom* is a statement that is taken to be true and serves as a premise or starting point for additional analysis or reasoning. Assembled here is a set of such statements – thoughts, sayings, or guideposts – that I've repeated again and again to remind myself of the *nature* of leadership. The intent is to help you step back from situations and yourself – to see through the eyes of an objective observer.

Axiom 1. Humility

Before you can learn you must first admit you don't already know.

Egos are challenging – both managing your own and navigating those of others. I try to laugh at myself at least once a day, but I'm not sure even that keeps me in check. I started keeping this axiom in my mind to remind me that the first step to growth and wisdom is humility. There is a delicate balance between confidence and humility. A truly humble person is secure and therefore confident.

The people who work with you, and observe you, will quickly recognize where you are with your ego, and will be reluctant to follow you if your ego is leading. I've seen too many leaders take credit for the work of their team – frequently with their own advancement in mind. I've also seen leaders receive a new role leading an organization and immediately take the position that everything that's previously been done is wrong and only they know the way forward. These examples are, as a minimum, discouraging and will likely cause a significant drop in productivity (see dialog on Maslow's hierarchy later under Compassion).

A better approach is to enter a new assignment with the intent to learn and understand by soliciting feedback from the people in the organization – chances are they have good ideas for improvement. They'll feel empowered by your desire to hear their ideas, and it affords you the opportunity to evaluate your staff. I've found that I learned the most about leadership from assignments where I had no subject matter expertise, and therefore had to rely on the members of my team to provide the core knowledge base.

At the same time it's important to keep in mind that you're only as good as the people who surround you. You need to surround yourself with the best people – those who are willing to disagree with you – trust them, and listen to their opinions. The power of diverse thought is only realized if it's brought to the table and heard. *None of us is as smart as all of us.* You might be the smartest person in the room, but you're not smarter than the room as a whole.

Axiom 2. Compassion

People are most productive when they're having fun.

Have you ever worked with a team where everything just "clicked" and the work became fun? It can be contagious, and the productivity skyrockets. People can't have fun if they don't feel safe.

Leadership is taking people to places they didn't believe they could go. What frequently stands in their way is fear or lack of confidence, and/or lack of vision or drive.

In simple terms, Mazlo's hierarchy[17] says we strive first to satisfy basic needs – things like food, shelter, an emotional sense of security. Once those are met, we eventually make our way to self-actualization – actually becoming everything we are capable of being. Some people habitually revisit the basic needs to reassure themselves that they're safe – for them the sense of security is unfortunately short-lived. So many, I suppose, live with a more or less constant underlying insecurity or fear – I believe to some extent we all do.

People are most willing to be led by someone they believe cares about them. If you provide an environment that lets folks feel safe (meet basic needs), they will then move on to self-actualization and productivity will increase. Drawing the most out of people – leadership – requires compassion.

Axiom 3. Courage

You don't lead by staying in the wake of others, but moving out of the wake means facing uncertainty.

Leading requires courage – plotting a course through potentially rough or uncharted waters and convincing others to follow you. It sometimes means moving forward facing into uncertainty, or making decisions that might be unpopular.

When faced with difficult situations (maybe even career impacting), I tried to keep a higher purpose in my mind – like what's the right ethical decision, or what's in the best interest of the company. I found, in general, if I did the right things for the right reasons I could sleep at night, and ultimately my career would look after itself. My belief in that reasoning provided me with the courage to face difficult decisions.

Axiom 4. Vision

It's difficult to navigate the path ahead by looking in the rear-view mirror.

Leaders also need vision. Here, by *vision*, I don't necessarily mean something ethereal or profound. Although some of the greatest leaders in history had profound vision for the future or the ultimate purpose of their company, the pace of change in today's business world may make grand visions short lived or so ethereal as to be essentially meaningless. "Being the greatest widget producer in the world" has less meaning if widgets become obsolete.

What I believe *is* required of a developing leader is a more operational approach to the concept of a vision. That is, the ability to read the environment, to anticipate the changes ahead, and to make the appropriate course selection or correction. The time horizon for the vision should be longer than your product-development cycles to be practical, but short enough to be tangible – something like 5-10 years.

Reading the environment is a matter of assembling information from multiple sources and organizing it by causal relationships – how do events relate to each other. This could be things like availability of raw materials, new or changing suppliers, new entries into your market (disrupters), your product mix, automation, or availability of labor.

The next step is developing scenarios (anticipate what could happen) based on the information and causal relationships – if event X occurs, what effect would it have on a series of other events. And finally then, determine the most likely scenario, or what outcomes are common to all scenarios. This will provide you with the basis for your vision and potential course selection.

Axiom 5. Drive

The fundamental motives are self-preservation and self-actualization.

Leaders must have drive – the ability to motivate themselves and others. I believe people are fundamentally motivated by either self-preservation (fear) or self-actualization. I argued above that leaders should make an effort to remove fear, and I would further hold that self-actualization is a more powerful motive in the long term.

Consider the following two approaches to gain better performance from an employee:

- You're not meeting my expectations and I need to see better performance from you or there will be consequences.

- I believe in you and I know you're capable of more, and I want to help you reach even higher.

The first feels threatening and although it may motivate the employee in the short term, in the long term the employee will likely feel less of a sense of loyalty and will seek other employment options. The second, on the other hand, is encouraging the employee to reach for their full potential – self-actualization, and is likely to engender loyalty *and* higher performance.

The same holds from a broader organizational perspective. Helping people rise to a higher purpose will drive productivity.

Axiom 6. Intuition

Intuition grows with experience.

We sometimes discount the experience of our elders. After all, just because you've done something for a long time doesn't mean you've done it well. We can't let experience, taken at face value, stand in the way of innovation or improvement. "We've always done it this way," is not a good argument against change.

On the other hand, I believe there is tremendous value in the intuition gained from experience. What I mean by *intuition* here is the *rapid use of knowledge that is distilled from experience.*

I was once having a conversation with an equipment operator as he was monitoring a very large system. It had just been outfitted with a sophisticated set of sensors and displays. I commented on how this must have changed his job – made it easier for him to detect and react to potential problems.

He replied that he had been working on this piece of equipment for many years and could tell from the sound and the smell if it was performing properly, and that if he had to rely solely on the sensors, his reaction might be too late. We should seek improvements via technology without discounting the value of intuition.

It also reminds me of the widely reported "Miracle on the Hudson" where Captain Sullenberger and crew landed the plane on the Hudson River.[18] It is broadly held that it was the experience and intuition of the captain that served to avoid a catastrophic result.

In some cases, reaction time demands the use of intuition. And in other cases, the availability of data or the required analysis may make an intuitive approach more practical. In this usage, my thoughts on intuition are similar to making a "judgment call."

When I think of judgment, I think of sound decision-making. We devoted time in the previous section on Execution to talk about the formal process of decision-making – things like criteria, alternatives, and risks. Following that process will help ensure sound decision-making and judgment. It will further instill trust in you by both your employees and your bosses.

There are times, however, when leaders are called upon to make "judgment calls" – needing to formulate opinions and take action quickly. In these cases, as a minimum, I would consider as many alternatives and consequences as feasible within the time constraints.

Sometimes, in the heat of the moment, people present a problem with seemingly only one solution – they've boxed themselves in. This is a trap for leaders. There are always alternatives, and for each of the alternatives, there are consequences – both intended and unintended – that should be considered. *What could possibly go wrong?* I've found most often that failures of judgment can be tied to failure to consider consequences.

Many business decisions rely on the use of intuition. I found in these cases that there was tremendous value in listening to some of the senior members of my team for their ideas. Not that I would simply do what they thought was right, but to hear the stories of "what happened the last time we tried something like this," and to then formulate how I would use the information to navigate the path ahead.

Finally, one of the most important jobs of a leader is developing others. As you're developing other leaders, look for opportunities to enlist senior members of your organization as coaches or mentors. Not so the new leaders can *watch*, but so they can *do* and learn how to avoid and/or react to mistakes – develop intuition. People learn more from discovery than they do from being told.

Teaching someone to lead is like teaching someone to swim – you can show them a movie or give them a book to read, but if you throw them in a pool they drown anyway. You must get in the pool with them, and support them while they flounder, until they finally relax and float.

Axiom 7. Perspective

We measure ourselves based on our intentions – others measure us based on our actions.

Our intentions are conversations we have in our own heads – "self talk" – that we employ to rationalize the actions we take (or don't take). The reality is that no one *really* sees our intentions. Our actions are the evidence that's used to form judgments of us. The key point here is to continually ask yourself, "What message am I sending with my actions and is it what I intend?"

In my experience, the best way to approach this is to first, communicate your intention along with the action to be taken. And second, ensure that your intention is aligned with your action. I've always found that it's a good idea to test your communication on someone you trust to give you candid feedback. And ask explicitly, "What message do you receive from my action and does it match the communicated intent?"

Sometimes the simplest actions can matter. I always made a habit that when someone came into my office to talk with me, I left the distractions of my desk and moved to a chair next to them so that, by my action, they knew they had my attention.

Axiom 8. Natural Selection

"Natural Selection" applies to everything.

The idea that nature "selects" by first introducing a random variant was one of Darwin's many contributions,[19] and is widely accepted. The ability of the introduced variant to adapt, and the environment to adopt, determines its survival.

In a broader interpretation, the physics concept of least action[20] selecting the most likely outcome could be considered another example of natural selection – outcomes are subject to the conditions of the environment.

It's also human nature to be wary of, or even reject, that which is different. This is much like the human body when something foreign is introduced and white blood cells are dispatched to rid us of the invader.

A group of people in an organization operates in many ways like a single organism. The introduction of a change into a business environment, to a large extent, follows the same rules – survival of the change is dependent on the environment. The change could be a new leader, a new employee, or a change initiative.

The key is to understand the environment and recognize the need to condition the environment to accept the change – condition the "immune" system. This conditioning is a matter of effective communication.

We fear that which we don't understand. A transparent communication plan that removes uncertainty, and provides reassurance (see section on Compassion) will serve to alleviate fear and help condition the environment.

It's also important to recognize that *Change is only resisted if it's noticed.* I've often coached leaders that unless a transformative change is urgently warranted, it is perhaps better to lead a more gradual, evolutionary approach. There is far less disruption and lost productivity.

Axiom 9. Knowledge

Knowledge can be stored in people or in processes.

In science, knowledge is advanced through the formulation of a theory and the validation by experiment. Much like our discussion on Natural Selection above, the survival of a new theory is dependent on the reconciliation of the new theory with the existing body of knowledge in the science community. The theory is generally captured by some form of documentation – a symbolic representation by language or mathematics.

It is not my intent to pontificate on the theory of knowledge,[21] but rather to consider how a leader can encourage, capture, and maintain knowledge in a business environment. What I mean here is that in the evolution of a business of any kind, people will learn how to perform tasks and develop networks. They will navigate the learning curve and the organization respectively. They will naturally look for better or easier ways of performing tasks and will (if they feel safe in their jobs) teach others how to perform the tasks. They will instinctively apply "Natural Selection" to advance new ideas. Intellectual capital is one of the most important forms of value that a company can possess.

What's important is to teach your employees how to recognize improvement opportunities, and how to make, and capture the value of, improvements. They will then go out and improve everything else. The key is to encapsulate improvements in the form of processes that survive the inevitable turnover of employees.

Process documentation is generally part of an overall Quality Management System (QMS), and there are standards set forth by the International Organization for Standardization (ISO).[22] For example, ISO-9001 provides the standards for a quality management system. These standards are in many cases required on government contracts.

Some caution should be taken, however, in the implementation of such standards to ensure that the ambition does not exceed the ability of your organization. You don't want the goal of attaining a process documentation standard to adversely impact the accomplishment of revenue-generating work. A balance can, and should, be achieved.

I have, for example, observed large companies acquiring small companies, and in an effort to "integrate" the small company into the larger, the small company was "crushed" by the process bureaucracy. Many of the key employees left, and with their departure the intellectual capital, and therefore the value, was lost.

For that reason I offer here a caveat to driving process standards:

Standardization is the enemy of innovation.

The statement may seem obvious, but at times the desire to control variation or to drive standardization can smother innovation. You may have heard the old saying, "The nail that stands up gets beat down." It's important to determine where it is essential to have strict process adherence and where to allow people the freedom to test new ideas – *freedom within boundaries.* Once again, balance is key.

Axiom 10. Measurement

What gets measured gets done – but if you measure too much, nothing gets done.

We measure things to see the result of change or to influence an outcome. These are respectively lagging and leading indicators. We step on a scale to measure the result of our efforts to lose weight – an outcome or lagging indicator. A leading indicator would be the comparison of the calories we consume (or absorb) versus the calories we burn.

Another example can be seen in many of today's cars – the fuel efficiency monitor. The fuel gauge reports the fuel used versus fuel remaining – a lagging indicator. The fuel efficiency monitor reports your current rate of consumption in real time. This allows you to adjust your behavior to influence the outcome.

There is frequently a desire among leaders seeking to have a sense of control to measure too much, and to measure the wrong things. In some cases, this desire can lead to a focus on measurements instead of a focus on the work, and productivity will suffer.

Measurements should drive a decision or action, or influence a behavior. For any measurement you should ask yourself, "What action would I take if this measure changed or will this measure provide me with an opportunity to influence an outcome?" If the answer is negative, then the measure is likely a waste of time or, worse, might drive the wrong behavior. I once had a leader tell me as I was presenting a new score card that it was, "interesting, but irrelevant." Obviously not the response I'd hoped for, but a valuable lesson.

My tendency is to concentrate on what I consider to be the basic measurements of management – cost, schedule, scope, risk, and quality. And if I were to pick only one, it would be quality – eliminating defects can cure many ills. In fact, from a system perspective[23] these measurements are related. For example, changing scope will change cost and schedule, risks can impact cost and schedule, and quality can impact everything. These measurements are like looking through different view ports at a system.

Axiom 11. Norms

Norms must be displaced in order to be changed.

Peter Drucker once said, "Culture eats strategy for breakfast."[12] In my experience, culture is what happens when no one is looking – it's the accepted norms. What I believe Drucker meant by his statement is people act based on cultural norms, and a strategy that doesn't recognize this will likely fail.

So what determines culture and how can we influence it? What I mean by the statement *norms must be displaced in order to be changed* is that it is not sufficient to ask people to stop doing something. You must instead provide a new model of acceptable behavior, exemplify the model yourself, and reward the behavior in others – educate, exemplify, and enforce.

People will generally choose the path of least resistance – the one that provides the greatest reward for the least effort. The job of a leader is to align the reward and effort with the path to the goal, and / or to inspire people to choose the path to the goal, even though it may be more difficult and less rewarding, out of a sense of greater purpose.

Axiom 12. Uncertainty

Left with uncertainty, people will create the worst possible reality.

Underlying this statement is the idea that *reality is nothing more than an agreed to set of perceptions*. If people are operating only on perceptions (uncertainty), then their collective fears will lead them to create the worst possible reality. This phenomenon is responsible in part for mass hysteria, and can severely impact productivity in a business environment.

The key to preventing this is consistent, regular, and transparent communication at all levels. It should be built into your management system, and accompanied by regular feedback mechanisms – like round-table meetings with employees, and/or tapping employee networks, to hear and answer concerns. The two-way dialog promotes trust and alleviates fear.

Once again, balance is warranted. The value of any communication must be greater than the disruption it causes. The goal here is to provide facts with compassion and sincerity that displace uncertainty and alleviate concerns.

Final Thoughts

This book was written as a companion guide for developing leaders. It's based on my experience as a leader, mentor, and lecturer. The goal, and my desire, is for this book to help developing leaders through what I saw as challenges during my own development and to provide them with tools to use, and distilled lessons to turn to, as they encounter challenges of their own. And remember, leadership is an emotional response – it's about how you make other people feel. Lead with your heart and people will follow.

About the Author

Michael currently lectures at the University of Washington's Milgard Business School. He retired as a vice president from a major engineering and manufacturing company where he had the opportunity to lead in multiple disciplines including engineering, program management, finance, and operations; and has also had careers as a theoretical physicist and chef. He earned a Ph.D. in physics from Kent State University and has completed executive education courses at

Wharton and the Brookings Institution, and has 19 publications in refereed journals.

Through multiple careers Michael has practiced, observed, mentored, and taught leadership at every level. His hope is to bring these experiences to developing leaders in a practical format.

Notes and References

[1] For more information on the term VUCA see for example US Army Heritage & Education Center, "VUCA", https://usawc.libanswers.com, and references therein.

[2] An *axiom* is a statement that is taken to be true and serves as a premise or starting point for additional analysis or reasoning – commonly held truths.

[3] Cuddy, A.J.C., Kohut, M., and Neffinger, J. (2013). Connect, Then Lead. *Harvard Business Review*, July – August.

[4] This was a conversation with Bill Grace of the Center for Ethical Leadership. Refer to http://www.ethicalleadership.org for more information.

[5] Benjamin Zander, for more information see: https://www.benjaminzander.org.

[6] For more information see Wharton Executive Education, University of Pennsylvania, https://executiveeducation.wharton.upenn.edu.

[7] Refer to Brookings Executive Education, https://www.brookings.edu/executive-education for more information.

[8] There are several good finance books available. One example is: A. A. Groppelli and Ehsan Nikbakht (2000). *Finance.* Hauppauge, NY: Barron's Educational Series, Inc.

[9] Porter, Michael E. (1980). *Competitive Strategy: Techniques for Analyzing Industries and Competitors.* New York, NY: The Free Press.

[10] Kaplan, R.S. and Norton, D. P. (2008). Mastering the Management System. *Harvard Business Review,* January.

[11] See for example: Luecke, R. (2005). *Strategy: Create and Implement the Best Strategy for Your Business.* Boston, MA: Harvard Business School Press.

[12] This is a quote that has been attributed to Peter Drucker. See also: Coffman, C., & Sorensen, K. (2013). *Culture eats strategy for lunch: The secret of extraordinary results, igniting the passion within.* Denver, CO: Liang Addison Press.

[13] Kotter, J. P. et al (1998). *Harvard Business Review on Change.* Boston, MA: Harvard Business School Press.

[14] See for example Program Management Institute at: https://www.pmi.org.

[15] For more information see respectively: Myers-Briggs, https://www.myersbriggs.org; Birkman, https://birkman.com; Herrmann Brain Dominance, https://www.thinkherrmann.com; and Insights, https://www.insights.com.

[16] This thought was introduced to me in a brief conversation with a former colleague whose name I can't recall.

[17] See for example: Maslow, A. H. (2000). *The Maslow business reader* (D. C. Stephens, Ed.). New York: Wiley.

[18] Refer to Wikipedia. *US Airways Flight 1549.* https://en.m.wikipedia.org/wiki/US_Airways_Flight_1549, and references therein.

[19] See for example: Darwin, C. R., & Ghiselin, M. T. (2006). *On the origins of species: By means of natural selection or the presevation of favoured*

races in the struggle for life. Mineola: Dover Publications.

[20] Refer to Wikipedia. *Principle of Least Action.* https://en.wikipedia.org/wiki/Principle_of_least_action.

[21] The context for what I'm referring to here as knowledge is most closely related to the work of W. Edwards Deming. Refer to The Deming Institute at: https://deming.org/.

[22] The International Organization for Standardization (ISO) can be found at: https://www.iso.org/home.html.

[23] This is again referring to the work of W. Edwards Deming. See for example: Deming, W. E. (1993). *The new economics for industry, government, education.* Cambridge, MA: Massachusetts Institute of Technology, Center for Advanced Engineering Study.

Made in United States
Troutdale, OR
12/05/2023